FOR THE GRANDMOTHER WHO HAS EVERYTHING

A Funny Book for Grandmothers

Bruce Miller and TeamGolfwell

This is the fourth book in the *For Someone Who Has Everything* series.

Cover by Queen Graphics. All images are from Creative Commons or Shutterstock

ISBN 9798417776250 (Amazon paperback)

ISBN 9798417790645 (Amazon hardback)

ISBN 9781991161611 (Ingram Spark Paperback)

ISBN 9781991161628 (Ingram Spark eBook)

Recipes. "If God had intended us to follow recipes, He wouldn't have given us grandmothers."

>--Linda Henley

A lovely blend. "Grandmothers are a delightful blend of laughter, caring deeds, wonderful stories and love."

>-- Anon.

A few more definitions of grandmother. Besides being all the nice things in the previous lovely blend paragraph, she is,

- Like mother but without the rules.

- A glamorous woman with grandchildren who is far too fabulous and gorgeous to be called Grandma.

- Excellent cook

- Giver of the world's greatest hugs

- A great listener

- Like mom only cooler

- A mother that has been promoted and possesses a wealth of knowledge and wisdom and cakes too

- Someone who is always there when you need them

- Always puts others first

- Gives the best advice

- A kind caring woman with a big heart

- Licensed to spoil

- Keeper of snacks and secrets

- Grandmas are moms with lots of frosting

- Loves you unconditionally

Just right. "Most grandmothers have just the right touch of the funny and the mischievous."

— Helen Thomson

Grandmother's childhood. A grandmother was telling her little granddaughter what her own childhood was like,

"We used to skate outside on a pond. I had a swing made from a tire; it hung from a tree in our front yard. We rode our pony. We picked wild raspberries in the woods."

The little girl was wide-eyed, taking this in. At last, she said, "I sure wish I'd gotten to know you sooner!"

-- Anon.

Way too cool. "They call me 'JoJo' cause I'm way too cool to be called grandmother."

-- Anon.

What's another name for grandmother?

Here are just a few,

Memaw (common in southern US states)

Nanny (taken to men sensible and sweet)

Nonna (grandmother in Italian)

Abuela (grandmother in Spanish)

Glamma (Short for glamorous and fabulous)

Lola (Grandmother in Filipino)

Baba (common in Slavic countries)

Gram (laid back casual grandmother)

Insta Gram (social media savvy grandmother)

Bibi (Grandmother in Swahili)

Mimsy (Grandmother who is intriguing and interesting)

Avó (Grandmother in Portuguese)

Babushka (Old fashioned Russian grandmother)

Gam Gam (a very cool grandmother)

Oma (Grandmother in German)

Funma (a grandmother who is too much fun!)

Yaya (Grandmother in Greek)

Cha-Cha (Grandmother who always dances)

Granny Pie (a grandmother who is as sweet as a piece of pie)

Ouma (Grandmother in Afrikaans)

Mémé (French Canadian grandmothers)

Nai Nai (Chinese grandmother)

Big Momma (a grandmother who is the boss and leads the family)

Gigi (a name that's easy for babies to say)

Bedstemoder (Grandmother in Danish)

TuTu (common in Hawaii – Tutu Wahine)

Savta (Grandmother in Hebrew)

Bella (a beautiful and attractive grandmother)

Bomma (Dutch grandmother)

Birdy (an outdoorsy grandmother)

WWII story. "Late 1944 in The Netherlands, my grandmother was busy cooking and paid no attention to the SS fighting of GI's in her yard until a bullet flew through her pan.

She put the pan away stepped into the yard yelling in German, "Go and play somewhere else!" She had an excellent German accent and according to her, they left.

I believed her when she told me that and still do. When the GI's had chased the SS past the German border 2 miles further, her war was finished.

My grandmother from then on interned 3 or 4 GI's in her home for the rest of the war. The GI's went to the front in Germany for a few weeks and what was left returned to my grandmother's hotel with the shoes from their fallen comrades (my uncle had no shoes left because of the war).

Loved that story from my grandmother."

-- Anon

A grandmother reports she loves this riddle -- and it's one of her grandkids' favorites too.

Where do Bees use the bathroom?

At the BP station.

Logical.

Boy aged 4: Dad, I've decided to get married.

Dad: Wonderful; do you have a girl in mind?!

Boy: Yes… grandma! She said she loves me, I love her, too… and she's the best cook and storyteller in the whole world!

Dad: That's nice, but we have a small problem there!

Boy: What problem?!

Dad: She happens to be my mother. How can you marry my mother!

Boy: Why not?! You married mine!

Not dead yet. I'm at that age where my mind still thinks I'm 29, my humor suggests I'm 12, and my body keeps asking if I'm sure I'm not dead yet.

-- Anon.

Granddaughter speaks her mind. I didn't know if my granddaughter had learned her colors yet, so I decided to test her. I would point out something and ask what color it was. She would tell me and always she was correct. But it was fun for me, so I continued.

At last, she headed for the door, saying sagely, "Grandma, I think you should try to figure out some of these yourself!"

-- Unknown

Tired. "I am really tired of babysitting my mother's grandkids right now."

-- a tired mom.

Balance. I see people about my age mountain climbing, but I feel good getting my leg through my underwear without losing balance.

-- Anon.

Misunderstood. My five-year-old grandson couldn't wait to tell his grandpa about the movie we had watched on television, "20,000 Leagues Under the Sea." The scenes with the submarine and the giant octopus had kept him wide-eyed. In the middle of the telling, my husband interrupted Mark, "What caused the submarine to sink?"

With a look of incredulity Mark replied, "Grandpa, it was the 20,000 leaks!!"

-- Unknown

Grandmothers learn fast. Why are grandmas excellent at learning different languages so quickly?

They are always "grandma-tically" correct.

Grandmothers feel what grandchildren feel. I know, most of you know this but if anyone ever doubts you, know that scientists have scanned grandmothers' brains while they're viewing photos of their young grandchildren.

"What really jumps out in the data is the activation in areas of the brain associated with emotional empathy," says James Rilling, Emory professor of anthropology and lead author of the study.

"That suggests that grandmothers are geared toward feeling what their grandchildren are feeling when they interact with them. If their grandchild is smiling, they're feeling the child's joy. And if their grandchild is crying, they're feeling the child's pain and distress." [1]

"Many of them also said how nice it is to not be under as much time and financial pressure as they were when raising their children," Rilling says. "They get to enjoy the experience of being a grandmother much more than they did being parents." [2]

Grandma's love. "One time, grandma told me that she would always love me, even if at times, I don't love myself.

"I don't really know what all that means but I think it means she loves me a whole lot."

— Sophia Carter-Parker, "Ready, Set, Go to Grandma's"

A joke. My grandson was visiting one day when he asked, "Grandma, do you know how you and God are alike?"

I mentally polished my halo while I asked, No, how are we alike?"

"You're both old," he replied.

    -- Anon.

Where's grandma? "My grandmother started walking five miles a day when she was sixty. She's ninety-seven now, and we don't know where the hell she is."

    -- Ellen DeGeneres

Amazing. "It's funny what happens when you become a grandparent. You start to act all goofy and do things you never thought you'd do. It's terrific."

-- Unknown.

Face piercing. "After I got my nose pierced, my grandmother looked at me and said, 'Well you used to be my favorite grandchild.'"

-- Anon.

Grandma was an attractive lady. Back in the early 1980s, my uncle was working as a bartender in New York City in a very well-known restaurant/nightspot. My grandma had gone up from her home in Florida on a late afternoon flight to spend the weekend with her son in New York.

When she arrived, her son was still at work, so she went to my uncle's restaurant and had a seat at the end of the bar to wait for him to get off work.

She sat there alone for a while, chatting with my uncle the bartender when he had a moment, but mostly waiting alone.

Eventually, my uncle walked over to her with a huge smile and a glass of extremely expensive champagne. A gentleman at a nearby table had seen the very beautiful woman sitting alone at the bar and sent over the glass.

Grandma turned to thank the man, and to her surprise, it was Prince Egon von Furstenberg, having a late dinner with his wife Diane and a group of friends.

Not bad for a country girl raised on a farm in rural Florida.

-- Anon.

Grandmothers and roses are just the same.

Each is God's masterpiece with different names.

-- Anon.

Diapers. My wife & I were keeping our young grandson for an afternoon. My wife said we were short of diapers and requested I go to the nearby Osco Drug Store to buy some additional ones.

I located a female clerk about 20-years-old at the store and asked which aisle I could find diapers. She responded, "adult or baby?"

Stylish. "I have always admired stylishly confident women who dress with great authority. This lifelong love of elegance began with the humble wardrobe of my late grandmother Mrs. Bennie Frances Davis."

-- Andre Leon Talley, American fashion journalist, stylist, creative director, and editor-at-large of Vogue magazine

Blessed are the grandparents. "Blessed are those who spoil and snuggle, hug and hope, pray and pamper, for they shall be called grandparents."

-- Anon.

Unimpressed. "I've had lots of kids come up and ask for my autograph. I've also had a grandmother stop me and ask me if I know a good place to buy underwear."

-- Prince William

Compensation. "Grandchildren are God's way of compensating us for growing old."

— Mary H. Waldrip

I'm not spoiling them. "I don't intentionally spoil my grandkids. It's just that correcting them often takes more energy than I have left."

— Gene Perret

Riddle. Try this one on your grandkids. At a four-legged table, there is one grandma, two mothers, two daughters, and a granddaughter. How many legs are under the table?

A. There are 10 legs under the table in total. We have a grandmother (who is also a mother), her daughter (both a mother and a daughter), and her granddaughter (a daughter and granddaughter). This is how we have 6 legs under the table plus the 4 legs of the table equal 10.

The lines on her face. "When she smiles, the lines in her face become epic narratives that trace the stories of generations that no book can replace."

— Curtis Tyrone Jones

I'd do it all again if… "I would love to go back and travel the road not taken, if I knew at the end of it, I'd find the same set of grandkids."

— Robert Brault

Birthdays. My grandmother may not be on Facebook, but she still remembers everyone's birthday.

-- Anon.

We all need that one person. "We should all have one person who knows how to bless us despite the evidence, Grandmother was that person to me."

— Phyllis Theroux, Journalist, columnist, humorist, and children's book author.

"Becoming a grandparent is a second chance. For you have a chance to use all the things you learned the first time around and may have made mistakes on. It's all love and no discipline. There's no thorn in the rose."

— Dr. Joyce Brothers

Nature of grandmothers. "Grandmothers always have time for you when everyone else is too busy."

-- Anon.

Grace. "It is as grandmothers that our mothers come into the fullness of their grace."

— Christopher Morley

If mama ain't happy...

Ain't nobody happy!

If grandma ain't happy...

RUN!

-- Anon.

Thank you, Grandma! "I went to college on a classical piano scholarship. My grandmother made me practice one full hour a day. Every day.

"Man, I thought all she wanted was for me not to have any fun. Next thing you know, you have a career in music. Now, not everybody's going to go on and be Mozart or Michael Jackson. But music makes you smarter."

-- Jamie Foxx, Academy award-winning actor

Diets

Grandma: How's your diet going"

Grandson: Ok

Grandma: Here's some banana bread and ice cream to take home.

You've learned. "You make all your mistakes with your own children so by the time your grandchildren arrive, you know how to get it right. Plus, once you turn fifty, you kind of stop caring what others think."

-- Liz Fenton, Author

Mother-in-law. A little boy was very excited about the arrival of his maternal grandmother. When she came in the door, the little boy rushed up to his granny totally excited she was finally here.

After welcoming her, the young boy was still overly excited, and his grandmother asked him why. "Daddy is going to perform the trick he promised."

"Oh, what trick is he going to do?" Grandmother asked.

"He said he'd climb the walls if you ever came visiting!"

(Dad will be walking strangely for a while and hopefully will be recovering soon!)

The Decider of fate. "Grandma was the decider of my fate. She shaped my life, without of course knowing what my life would be. She taught me many things that I was going to need to know, without either of us knowing I would need to know them."

-- Wendell Berry, Novelist, poet

Grandma means,

Kiss giving

Boo-boo fixing

Candy buying

Fun supplying

An army. "Having a grandmother is like having an army. This is a grandchild's ultimate privilege. Knowing that someone is on your side, always, unconditionally, whatever the details. Even when you are wrong. Especially then, in fact. A grandmother is both a sword and a shield."

-- Fredrik Backman

The stork of course. Little Peter and little Johnny asked their grandma, "How are children born Granny?".

"The Stark brings them in his beak my children", said Granny.

Little Peter and little Johnny looked at each other and Little Jonny whispered, "What do you think Peter, shall we tell her?"

"No, no," said Peter, "Leave her in her innocence"

Grandma's surprise story. I was sitting at the kitchen table at Grandma's house. Grandpa was out running errands with Dad.

After killing about 3/4 of a bottle of potent wine between us, Grandma loosened up and got down to brass tacks. I was 17, below legal drinking age except at Grandma's kitchen table, which was still 17.

She asked me about my love life. Do I have a girlfriend? Did I find a nice Polish girl? My grandparents were already in their late 60's. She said don't wait too long, because she wanted to still be around to "dance at my wedding." She married Grandpa at 16 and had my father at 18, which wasn't uncommon in the 1920s.

Then...

She leaned forward conspiratorially, and said, you know, she and grandpa "still put notches on their bedpost."

I am still alive today because I managed to not choke to death on a cookie I was eating at that moment. Go ahead Grandma, do it. Testify. You just gotta love Grandma.

As it turned out, grandma did get to dance at my wedding.

    -- Anon.

Walking with Grandma.

I like walking with grandma

Her steps are short like mine

She doesn't say now hurry up

She always takes her time.

I like to walk with grandma

Her eyes see things like mine do

Wee pebbles bright, a funny cloud

Half hidden drops of dew.

Most people have to hurry

They do not stop and see

I'm glad that God made grandma

Unrushed and young like me.

-- Anon.

Grandmothers are more active than you think. 43% exercise or play sports. 28% volunteer on a regular basis. Also 18% dance. [3]

Grandmother texting grandson.

- Can you get me some long-life milk on your way around, please?

  o Bit optimistic. You're 87.

- YOUR'E out of the will.

  -- Anon.

Riddle. Try this on a grandchild. Suppose your grandchild is on his or her way to visit you, and you live at the end of the valley. It's your birthday, and the grandchild wants to give you the cakes the grandchild made.

Between the grandchild's house and your house, he or she must cross 7 bridges, and as it goes in the land of make-believe, there is a hungry troll under every bridge! There is no other way to go, and the child must cross over the 7 bridges.

Each troll, quite rightly, insists that anyone who wants to cross the bridge must pay the troll a toll before crossing the bridge. The toll for each bridge is one-half of the cakes being carried, and the child must give each troll half of the cakes the child is carrying, but as they are kind trolls, they each give you back a single cake.

How many cakes do you have to leave home with to make sure that you arrive at Grandma's with exactly 2 cakes?

A. You leave your home with two cakes since at each bridge you are required to give half of your cakes, and you receive one back. This leaves you with 2 cakes after every bridge!

Outspoken grandmother. My neighbors' family had a huge fight yesterday. Allegedly it started when their son introduced his girlfriend and granny responded: 'See what happens when you don't pray?'

Different. "A grandchild is different. Gone are the bonds of guilt and responsibility that burden the maternal relationship. The way to love is free."

-- Kate Morton

A haven. "A grandmother is a safe haven."

— Suzette Haden Elgin

Embarrassed! "Steven's words slush together as he gets to his feet. 'Crossing this one off the bucket list.' Then he unbuckles his belt and grabs the waist of his pants—yanking the suckers down to his ankles—tighty-whities and all.

Every guy in the car holds up his hands to try to block the spectacle. We all groan and complain.

'Put your pants on. My eyes! They burn!' But our protests fall on deaf ears. Steven is a man on a mission. Wordlessly, he squats and shoves his lily-white butt out the window—mooning the gaggle of grannies in the car next to us.

I bet you thought this kind of stuff only happened in movies.

He grins while his ass blows in the wind for a good ninety seconds, ensuring optimal viewage.

Then he pulls his slacks up, turns around, and leans out the window, laughing. 'Enjoying the full moon, ladies?'

Wow! Steven usually isn't the type to visually assault the elderly.

Without warning, his crazy cackling is cut off. He's silent for a beat, then I hear him choke out a single strangled word.

'Grandma?'

Still totally embarrassed, I looked at Steven and I'm pretty sure (even to this day) it's the funniest darn thing I've ever seen as all of us collapse back into our seats, laughing hysterically."

(Steven learned a lifelong lesson that day)

— Emma Chase, excerpt from "Tied"

Gold in her heart. "A grandmother is someone with silver in her hair and gold in her heart."

-- Unknown

Obits. A grandson asked, "Granny, why do you read obituaries every day?"

"Don't worry, I just want to see who is single again."

    -- Anon.

My grandmother told me this one. "When you drink vodka over ice, it can give you kidney failure.

When you drink rum over ice, it can give you liver failure.

When you drink whiskey over ice, it can give you heart problems.

When you drink gin over ice, it can give you brain problems.

Apparently, ice is really bad for you. Warn all your friends."

    -- Anon.

Walk the walk. "You never know the love of a grandparent until you become one."

    -- Anon.

Experienced. "Grandparents are voices of the past and the door to the future. They provide us with the wisdom from a lifetime of experience that should never be undervalued."

-- Anon.

Grandparent's auto phone message.

"Good morning. . .. At present we are not at home but, please leave your message after you hear the beep. Beeeeeppp ...

If you are one of our children, dial 1 and then select the option from 1 to 5 in order of "arrival" so we know who it is.

If you need us to stay with the children, press 2.

If you want to borrow the car, press 3.

If you want us to wash your clothes and do the ironing, press 4.

If you want the grandchildren to sleep here tonight, press 5.

If you want us to pick up the kids at school, press 6.

If you want us to prepare a meal for Sunday or to have it delivered to your home, press 7.

If you want to come to eat here, press 8.

If you need money, dial 9.

If you are going to invite us to dinner, or, take us to a restaurant, start talking - we are listening!"

Just plain fun. "If becoming a grandmother was only a matter of choice, I should advise every one of you straight away to become one. There is no fun for old people like it."

— Hannah Whithall Smith

Favorite. "My favorite thing at grandpa's house is grandma."

-- a grandson

Pun. My grandmother told my grandfather he needs a new hearing aid, but he would not listen.

5 true facts why grandmothers are essentially very important. [4]

The first is obvious. You wouldn't be here without your grandmother. The current scientific consensus is that women are born with a single supply of eggs that will last their whole lifetime. These eggs are formed while the female fetus is still in her mother's womb. That means that your mother's egg that created you was formed inside your grandmother's body before your mother herself was even born. Your grandmother carried part of you while she carried your mother.

2. Grandmothers provide guidance, wisdom, and insight. Seniors are often portrayed as being stuck in the past, but the actual reality is that they've done a lot of learning and adapting over the years. Many children and teenagers feel grandma is the person to ask when they have a problem they don't know how to solve.

3. Grandmothers often play a big role in caring for grandkids. No parent can do it all. Grandmothers can help make this balancing act a little easier by caring for their grandchildren some of the time.

4. A grandmother is a loving, trustworthy adult figure that kids can turn to. When parents and kids disagree or kids feel they need another opinion, many turn to grandmother for advice, hugs, or simply just a listening ear.

5. Grandmothers help their grandkids create memories that will be treasured forever. Many people have the best memories in their lives when being with their grandmother.

Studies have also shown, "Although not every set of grandparents is alike, maintaining a close relationship between grandparents and their grandchildren is good for everyone involved.

"In fact, adult grandchildren who have a close relationship with their grandparents are less likely to have symptoms of depression than adults who don't have this kind of relationship (Moorman & Stokes, 2014).

"This is true for the grandparents as well, who are also less likely to have depressive symptoms if they have close relationships with their grandchildren.

"In fact, research suggests that providing some kind of care for a grandchild—by babysitting on the weekends, for example—is related to longer life expectancy for the grandparent when compared to grandparents who don't take care of their grandchildren or adults of the same age who aren't grandparents at all (Hilbrand, Coall, Gerstorf, & Hertwig, 2017). [5]

Difficult report. A grandson in grade school is writing a report for school on childbirth and asks his grandmother, "How was I born?"

She awkwardly answers, "You were found under a cabbage leaf."

"Oh, well, how were you and Daddy born?"

"Oh, we were found under a cabbage leaf too."

The grandson continues writing, "This report has been very difficult to write due to the fact that there hasn't been a natural childbirth in my family for three generations."

-- Anon.

Grand angels. "Sometimes our grandmas and grandpas are like grand-angels."

— Lexie Saige

Amazing. "My grandmother is over eighty and still doesn't need glasses. Drinks right out of the bottle."

-- Henny Youngman

"A Pullover" A policeman is driving down the freeway when he looks over and spots a granny knitting whilst balancing the steering wheel with her knees.

He pulls alongside the granny, and angrily shouts "pull over!"

The granny shouts back, "No, it's a scarf."

Nana. "For myself, one of the sweetest words I have ever heard is 'Nana.'"

-- Zelda Rosenbaum, Producer

Fast baker. My grandma bakes cookies the fastest I've ever seen in my life! She does it in "Nana seconds!"

Collecting birthdays. "My grandmother lived to 104 years old, and part of her success was she woke up every morning to a brand-new day. She said every morning is a new gift. Her favorite hobby was collecting birthdays."

-- George Takei, Actor

Be a gentleman. "My Grandmother would say, 'Make sure you look good. Make sure you speak well. Make sure you remain that Southern gentleman that I've taught you to be.'"

-- Jamie Foxx

Grandmother

"Her words

are like a golden thread that binds our family.

Her wisdom,

like an art that shares so generously.

Her feelings

like a quilt that warms us like no other.

The hands

of one so dear the one we call Grandmother."

-- Sheria S. Barnett

You can do anything you want to. "I come from a long line of strong and confident women out of New Orleans. My grandmother and great-grandmother were women who ran their homes and were leaders in their communities. I was never taught that there was anything that I couldn't do, and I believed that."

-- Stephanie Allain, Successful independent Hollywood film producer

Silly joke. "My grandma has ingrained this silly joke in my head.

What did one strawberry say to the other strawberry?

If you weren't so fresh last night, we wouldn't be in this jam!"

-- Unknown

Two stories about grandma. Ah, Grandma, Grandma, Grandma... she was always saying funny stuff. Here are two stories.

The first is about Basic Instinct. For those of you who don't know, this was a film that starred Sharon Stone, which had a famous scene in it, where Shazza crosses her legs during a Police interview, and you get a fleeting glimpse of her downstairs lady bits. She was wearing no knickers while filming. "Minge out" was scandalous at the time.

Anyway, my grandma and grandad were around at Mum's house for tea, and grandma said, "Have you seen that movie 'Basic Instinct?' Ooh, it's DISGUSTING! ...we've seen it twice now."

That cracked us all up (sorry, no pun initially intended, but there it is), and it was brought up regularly over the years.

The second story is about their names. They both had the first initial 'F' and the surname 'Hall'. In our Yorkshire accent, we tend to drop the 'H' a lot, meaning their names sound like "Eff 'all".

One story about that was, my grandma had cause to go to the bank, angry about poor service and ready to complain. They (she and Grandad) had a joint account, and the Teller asked for her husband's name.

"F. 'all", she replied.

The teller gave her a funny look, and asked, "All right - so what's your name then?"

"That's F. 'all, an' all!" answered Grandma, getting exasperated, as this was a complaint, after all.

"Madam, I am trying to help you - what name is the account in, please?"

"F. AN' F. 'ALL!" huffed my grandma, but, sounding somewhat like "effing eff all", the teller thought my Grandma was being unnecessarily angry and sweary, and said, "Well! There's no need to be like that!"

My Grandma had to take a breath, and say calmly and clearly, "the account name is F and F Hall".

After which, the teller apologized for getting the wrong end of the stick, thinking my grandma was swearing at her, when she wasn't. It sounded inappropriate, but it wasn't really! I never actually heard my grandma swear ever, so it was funny when she told us the story.

-- Anon.

No regrets. "You will never look back on life and think, 'I've spent too much time with my grandchildren.'"

-- Anon.

A joke. Johnny was in kindergarten and his teacher assigned homework asking him to learn the first five letters of the ABCs. He goes home and asks his mom who's cooking, "What's the first letter of the ABC's?"

Mom is upset and busy trying to get dinner ready and it's not going very well, and she says, "SHUT UP... I'M COOKING!"

Johnny then walks over to his sister who is singing in the bathroom. "What's the 2nd letter of the ABC's?"

She's excited to be going out later so she says, "I'm ready to go I'm ready to go!"

Johnny then walks over to his brother who's watching batman on TV and asks, "What's the 3rd letter of the ABC's?"

His brother says, "Nu nu nu nu batman!"

Johnny then asks his dad who is watching football in another room and asks, "Dad what's the 4th letter of the ABC's?"

Dad says, "95 HIT EM HARD!"

Johnny then goes to the kitchen where his grandmother is cooking buns and asks her, "What's the 5th letter of the ABC's?"

She says, "MY BUNS ARE RED HOT RED HOT!"

The next day, the teacher says to her class, "Can any of you tell me the first letter of the ABC's?"

Johnny, of course, raises his hand and the teacher calls on him then he says, "SHUT UP I'M COOKING!"

The teacher raises an eyebrow and says, "Young man are you ready to go to the principal's office?"

Johnny says, "I'm ready to go I'm ready to go!" and he walks to the principal's office. The principal asks him, "What's your name son?"

Johnny says, "Nu nu nu nu batman!"

The old-time principal says, "Oh! You're looking for a paddling. How many do you want?"

Johnny says, "95 HIT EM HARD!"

Then Johnny immediately runs out of the principal's office yelling, "MY BUNS ARE RED HOT RED HOT!"

Don't mess with grandma. "As I learned from growing up, you don't mess with your grandmother."

-- Prince William

Smart mosquitoes. When my grandson, Charlie, and I entered our vacation cabin, we kept the lights off until we were inside to keep from attracting pesky insects. Still, a few fireflies followed us in. Noticing them before I did, Billy whispered "It's no use, Grandma. The mosquitoes are coming after us with flashlights."

-- Unknown

Interesting statistics on grandmothers (and grandfathers who are included in the percentages).

Almost all said, they like to spend time with their grandkids.

60% live close to their grandchildren.

46% wish they could live even closer.

70% see the kids at least once a week.

66% travel with their grandkids.

81% have their grandkids for part or all their summer vacation.

55% play video games with their grandchildren. [6]

What this grandmother liked. "My grandmother was a very simple woman. She didn't want a whole lot. My grandmother wanted to go to church and Sunday school every Sunday. She wanted to be in Bible study every Wednesday. The other days, she wanted to be on a fishing creek.

"I respect her deeply as she by herself raised her nine kids and raised my mom's three."

-- Shannon Sharpe, AFL Denver Broncos All-Pro Tight End

Bad influence? "They call me grandma since "partner in crime" makes me sound like a bad influence."

-- Anon

Babysitting Logic.

One evening a grandmother was babysitting her two granddaughters Annie and Betty and 8:00 PM rolled around.

"Okay, time for bed," she informed the two children who were playing in the den.

"Why?" Annie asked (aged 6). "It's so early!"

"Your father said your bedtime is 8:00," the grandmother said.

Betty (aged 4½) replied, "You don't have to listen to him."

"Why not?" the grandmother asked.

"Because you're his mother!"

In our hearts forever. "Grandmas hold our tiny little hands for just a little while, but our hearts forever."

-- Anon

Good looks.

Grandson: "Hi Grandmother, you are looking more beautiful than ever."

Grandmother: "You did have to inherit your good looks from someone."

Shakespeare. My grandparents took me on a vacation to Disneyworld. Grandma was excited for me when we boarded the plane, she said that I was lucky, because I got the "Shakespeare seat."

"Why is it the Shakespeare seat Grandma?"

"You are in seat 2-B, so it's the Shakespeare seat."

"Don't be silly Grandma. All the seats on an airplane are Shakespeare seats."

"How do you figure that?"

"Well, it's either seat 2-B or not 2-B."

> -- Anon.

Oh my! Who are you?! "A grandmother is the only one who pretends she doesn't know who you are on Halloween."

> -- Erma Bombeck

Grandmother always looked great. "My grandmother was probably the first person who I thought was beautiful. She was incredibly stylish, she had big hair, big cars. I was probably 3 years old, but she was like a cartoon character. She'd swoop into our lives with presents and boxes, and she always smelled great and looked great."

-- Tom Ford, fashion designer

"Grandmothers cannot be defined by age, appearance, or energy levels. We were just mothers who were incredibly blessed and became GRAND!"

-- Unknown

Grandma's remembered advice. "My dad was a very quiet person, and unbelievably tough. But my grandmother gave me my first look at negative thinking to bring about positive results. When I was just a little guy, anytime I came to my grandmother and said I wish for this or that, Grandma would say, 'If wishes were horses, beggars would ride.'"

-- Bobby Knight

Satisfying statistics.

- 72% think being a grandparent is the single most important and satisfying thing in their life.

- 63% say they can do a better job caring for grandchildren than they did with their own.

- 68% think being a grandparent brings them closer to their adult children.

- 90% enjoy talking about their grandkids to just about everyone. [7]

The oldest thing in the world. "My grandkids believe I'm the oldest thing in the world. And after two or three hours with them, I believe it, too."

-- Gene Perret, Comedy writer.

Wonderful. "Becoming a grandmother is wonderful. One minute you're just a mother. The next you're all wise and prehistoric."

-- Pam Brown

Make babies. A second grader came home from school and said to her grandmother, "Grandma, guess what? We learned how to make babies today."

Grandma, more than a little surprised, tried to keep her cool. "That's interesting," she said, "How do you make babies?"

"It's simple," replied the girl. "You just change "y" to "i" and add 'es'"

-- Unknown and a great joke for the English teacher

Born. "When a child is born, so are grandmothers."

-- Judith Levy, Actress

Silly riddles for grandkids.

- Why did the grandmother put wheels on her rocking chair?

  She wanted to rock and roll!

- I am pinched by grandmothers. Who am I?

  Cheeks!

- An easy one to ask grandkids. This person is the son of your grandparents, but he is not your uncle. Who is he?

  Your father!

Tough grandmother. "My grandmother was a very tough woman. She buried three husbands and two of them were just napping."

-- Rita Rudner, Comedian

Grandmother's sayings. "My grandmother had a great saying that always stuck with me, 'People don't care how much you know until they know how much you care.' "They've got to see it and feel it. And it's for real. And that's all. Be who you are."

-- Joe Manchin, United States Senator

Grandma texting

Grandmother: Your grandfather has just passed away LOL

Grandson: What do you mean, Grandma? LOL means "laughing out loud?"

Grandmother: Oh no! I thought that means "lots of love" I must hurry and text everyone back!

"Grandparents are there to help the child get into the mischief they haven't thought of yet."

"Me? Spoil them? I don't spoil my grandkids, I'm just very accommodating."

-- Unknown

Greatest cook. My grandmother was the greatest cook in the world. She could just go in there; the whole kitchen would look like a tornado hit it and then she'd come out with the best food. Then she'd sit at the table, and she wouldn't eat!

-- Edie Brickell, Singer, and songwriter

Grandparents Love. "When my grandmother got arthritis, she couldn't bend over and paint her toenails anymore. So, my grandfather does it for her all the time, even when his hands got arthritis too. That's love."

-- Mary, age 9

Morning coffee. A grandmother was surprised by her 7-year-old grandson one morning. He had made her coffee. She drank what was the worst cup of coffee in her life. When she got to the bottom, there were three of those little green army men in the cup. She said, "Honey, what are these army men doing in my coffee?"

Her grandson said, "Grandma, it says on TV, 'The best part of waking up is soldiers in your cup!'"

> -- Unknown

Impossible. "It's impossible for a grandmother to understand that few people, and maybe none, will find her grandchild as endearing as she does."

> -- Janet Lanese

Riddle. Why did the grandchildren stay up all night?

They wanted to see where the sun went. The next day, it dawned on them.

A poet's view. "Mom was terrible with young kids. My mom was a terrible parent of young children. And thank God - I thank God every time I think of it - I was sent to my paternal grandmother."

-- Maya Angelou

Love is free. "It's special, grandparents and grandchildren. So much simpler. Is it always so, I wonder? I think perhaps it is. While one's child takes a part of one's heart to use and misuse as they please, a grandchild is different. Gone are the bonds of guilt and responsibility that burden the maternal relationship. The way to love is free."

— Kate Morton

It might still happen. Oldest new grandmother - according to the Guinness World Records, the oldest first-time grandmother is Marianne Wallenberg who was 95 years old when her first grandson Joshua Fritz Wallenberg was born at Sinai Hospital, in Toronto. Marianne became the first-time grandmother when her son James and his wife Jacqueline gave birth to twins Joshua Fritz Wallenberg and Karina Diana Wallenberg. [8]

Grandmother's hearing aid. "I heard my grandmother talking to my dad about her new hearing aid. She said, "It's the most expensive one on the market. It cost me $4,000!"

"Wow! What kind is it?" my dad asked.

Grandmother replied, "It's 4:15pm."

-- Unknown

Enchantment. "A mother becomes a true grandmother the day she stops noticing the terrible things her children do because she is so enchanted with the wonderful things her grandchildren do."

-- Lois Wyse, Columnist

Of course! "One day, young Sarah girl was watching her mother make a roast sirloin of beef. She cut off the ends, wrapped it with string, seasoned it, and set it in the roasting dish.

Sarah politely asked her mum why she cut off the ends of the roast. Mum replied, after some thought, that it was the way that her mother had done it.

That night grandma came to dinner and Sarah and her mother asked why she had cut the end off of the roast before cooking. After some thought grandma replied, she cooked the meat the way her mother had done it.

Now great grandma was quite old and lived in a residential nursing home, so Sarah, her mom, and grandma went to visit her and again asked the very same question.

Great-grandma looked at them a bit surprised and said, 'So it would fit in the roasting dish, of course.'"

-- Gore Vidal

A gem. "The old are the precious gem in the center of the household."

-- Unknown

Granddaughter's tale about a back massager. "My grandmother is 83 and a very kind, thoughtful and sweet woman but she had problems with her back. So, we got her a full back massager that she puts on her recliner and it's electric and it helps her. She naively always refers to it as 'her vibrator.'

"I remember the time when my boyfriend came to Sunday dinner and mentioned he strained a muscle in his back. I will never forget the look on his face when my grandmother said, "Would you like me to fetch my vibrator from upstairs? It usually makes me feel better."

Old age. When you finally reach the point where you know a lot more than you did about life when you were younger, you begin to forget everything you know.

-- Unknown

"An hour with your grandchildren can make you feel young again. Any longer than that, and you start to age too quickly."

Saved mom. "My mom, Irmelin, taught me the value of life. Her own life was saved by my grandmother during World War II."

-- Leonardo DiCaprio, Actor

$50 is $50. A grandmother and her two grandchildren walked through the park every Sunday and always passed the helicopter rides. The grandkids asked, "Grandma, let's go for a ride. It's only $50!"

Grandma would always reply, "I know, I know kids, but that helicopter ride is $50! And $50 is $50."

On one Sunday, they passed the helicopter ride again and one of them said, "Grandma, you're 85 years old and if we don't take that ride with you not, we might not get another chance."

"Kids, that helicopter ride is $50 and $50 is $50." Grandma replied.

The helicopter pilot overheard them and said, "I'll take you all for a ride, and as long as you stay quiet for the whole ride, I won't charge you. But if any of you say one word, I'll charge you $50."

The kids and grandma agreed and up they went!

The pilot, however, wanted them to say something, so he made extra sharp turns, harrowing quick descents, and all kinds of fancy and dangerous maneuvers, yet no one said a word.

When they landed, the pilot said, "Heck, I did everything I could to make you yell out, but you didn't. I have to say I'm impressed."

The oldest grandchild spoke up, "I almost said something when grandma fell out but $50 is $50." Just then grandma landed using the parachute she had been given.

Look inside. "A grandparent is old on the outside, but young on the inside."

-- Unknown

Acceptance. "Our grandchildren accept us for ourselves, without rebuke or effort to change us, as no one in our entire lives has ever done, not our parents, siblings, spouses, friends — and hardly ever our own grown children."

— Ruth Goode, Writer, and editor

Better than all of them. "Uncles and aunts, and cousins, are all very well, and fathers and mothers are not to be despised; but a grandmother, at holiday time, is worth them all."

-- Fanny Fern, Novelist

Get out! A Florida grandmother was out shopping and, upon returning to her car, found four males in the act of stealing her vehicle.

She dropped her shopping bags and drew her handgun, proceeding to scream at the top of her lungs, "I have a gun, and I know how to use it! Get out of the car!"

The four men didn't wait for a second threat. They got out and ran like mad.

The lady, somewhat shaken, then proceeded to load her shopping bags into the back of the car and got into the driver's seat. She was so shaken that she could not get her key into the ignition.

She tried and tried, and then she realized why. It was for the same reason she had wondered why there was a football, a Frisbee, and two 12-packs of beer in the front seat.

A few minutes later, she found her own car parked four or five spaces along.

She loaded her bags into the car and drove to the police station to report her mistake.

The sergeant to whom she told the story couldn't stop laughing. He pointed to the other end of the counter, where four young men were reporting a carjacking by a mad, elderly woman described as white, less than five feet tall, with glasses, curly white hair, and a large handgun. [9]

The universal nature of grandmothers. When my grandmother first went to the United States from the Philippines, she had to go through customs. The customs officer asked her whether she had any dried fish, salted shrimp fry, or mangoes. Unaware that this was part of the routine inspection, my grandmother politely replied, "Had I known you wanted any, sir, I would have brought you some."

-- Unknown

Content and happy. "Going to see my grandparents was the highlight of my childhood summers. I was doted upon, admired, entertained, and overfed. I was never more content and happier."

— Carolyn Anthony

Grandma passes on her stories. The author of Frankenstein, Mary Shelley created a legendary character that has permeated and existed in all mediums of storytelling that continues to this day to inspire new bone-chilling tales. She was a grandmother to a single granddaughter to whom she passed her stories on and her stories are told among generations in her family line ever since. [10]

Sense of identity. "My grandmother lived with us. I picked up quite a bit of family lore and history from her, which was interesting."

-- John Hume, Irish politician

Grandmother makes the best of it. This is an interesting story.

"My gram had arrived at my house the evening before after a long flight. When I woke up the next morning, she was nowhere to be found. So, I jumped in my car and drove around town looking for her most of the morning.

After several hours I decide to take a lunch break at my favorite Mexican restaurant. I ordered my tacos and sat down at an empty table. When my food was done, I was served by an old lady in a sombrero. I looked up to thank her, and I see my gramma!

My gram was pretty jet-lagged, so early in the morning she decided to take a walk, and (of course) got lost with no cellphone or cash. She wandered into town just as stores were opening. She walked up to the friendliest-looking restaurant (my favorite Mexican restaurant) and (with her limited English) asked if she could stay there until I found her.

They misunderstood her and thought she wanted to work there. They gave her an apron and some dishcloths and pointed at the tables. She cleaned them up. Then they gave her a dish brush and pointed at the dishes, and she cleaned them. This continued until I found her.

I talked to the lovely Mexican couple who owned the restaurant and explained the situation and thanked them for their help. They offered my gram a part-time position to help open shop every morning for the rest of her stay and paid her a nice wage."

-- Anon.

What makes up grandma? "A grandmother is a little bit parent, a little bit teacher, and a little bit best friend."

-- Unknown

Energy. Sometimes I wish I had the wisdom of a 90-year-old, the body of a 20-year-old, and the energy of a three-year-old.

-- Anon.

Baking. "All my grandchildren bake. On a Saturday, Annabel's boys, Louis, and Toby, always bake. Louis makes a chocolate cake; Toby makes banana or lemon drizzle. They're 12 and 10, and they can do it totally on their own. My son's twin girls, Abby, and Grace are 14; they make birthday cakes and like to do it on their own with Mum out of the way.

-- Mary Berry

Close to heaven. "My grandmother made sure that I went to church every Sunday. And she'd come over and pick us boys up, and we would go to the Nazarene church. And back then, that was about as close to heaven as I ever got, because just the time to be able to spend with her, and she was very, very religious."

-- John Mellencamp, Singer-songwriter, painter, actor, and film director

Honor Grandmother

While we honor all our mothers

with words of love and praise.

While we talk about their goodness

and their kind and loving ways.

We should also think of Grandma

she's a mother too, you see…

For she mothered my dear mother

as my mother mothers me.

-- Unknown

Grandmother's cooking. "We believed in our grandmother's cooking more fervently than we believed in God. Her culinary prowess was one of our family's primal stories, like the cunning of the grandfather I never met, or the single fight of my parents' marriage. We clung to those stories and depended on them to define us. We were the family that chose its battles wisely, and used wit to get out of binds, and loved the food of our matriarch."

— Jonathan Safran Foer, Novelist

Beautiful. "Beautiful young people are accidents of nature. But beautiful grandmothers are works of art."

— Marjory Barstow-Greenbie, Author

Record for most generations alive. This is amazing. The most generations alive in a single-family are seven. The youngest great-great-great-great-grandparent is Augusta Bunge, and she is from the US and aged 109 years 97 days, followed by her daughter aged 89, her grand-daughter aged 70, her great-grand-daughter aged 52, her great-great-granddaughter aged 33, and her great-great-great-granddaughter aged 15 on the birth of her great-great-great-great-grandson on 21 January 1989. [11]

Conservative. "A conservative is someone who makes no changes and consults his grandmother when in doubt."

-- Woodrow Wilson, Former US President

Grammy's toilet brush joke. A grandmother told a joke - let's call her Grammy.

Grammy was walking down the street and her neighbor, let's call her Joyce, was heading towards her carrying her shopping but was walking kind of funny.

Naturally, Grammy asked if everything was okay and if she was alright. Did she had hurt herself?

"No, she said, "I'm okay. I've just bought one of those new toilet brushes, but I think I'm going to switch back to paper."

-- Anon.

Complete. "Grandma always made you feel she had been waiting to see just you all day and now the day was complete."

-- Marcy DeMaree

Cooking supper. "I tried cooking supper with wine tonight. Didn't go so well. After 5 glasses I didn't even know I was in the kitchen."

-- Anon.

Self-respect. "Self-respect is something that our grandparents (whether or not they had it), knew all about it. They had instilled in them, when they were young, a certain discipline, the sense that one lives by doing things that one does not particularly want to do, and putting any fears and doubts to one side, and weighing immediate comforts against the possibility of larger, even intangible, comforts."

— Joan Didion, American writer

A few interesting facts about grandparents.

- There are over 70 million grandparents in the nation.

- Grandparents represent one-third of the population and lead 37% of all U.S. households in this country.

- Grandparents make 45% of the nation's cash contributions to nonprofit organizations.

- 72% think being a grandparent is the single most important role in their lives.

- 2 million U.S. households are multigenerational. [12]

Grannie isn't scared. A state trooper stopped an 85-year-old woman and couldn't help but notice she had a concealed weapons license as well. So, he asked her, "Have any weapons, Ma'am?"

"Why yes I do. I have a Colt Python 357 magnum in the console, a Smith & Wesson 44 magnum in the glove compartment and a 38 special in my purse."

"LADY what are you scared of?" asked the trooper.

She said, "Not a darn thing."

The Years Fly By

You say the years fly by

Well, that I won't deny.

And here we are another year

I just want to say that you're a dear.

It doesn't matter what the age

It's just a number so don't engage

Just be yourself and keep living each day

You are the best Grandmother in every way.

If you are finding this birthday makes you blue

Let me sing a song just for you,

Happy Birthday Grandmother I do sing

All my love I do bring!

-- Catherine Pulsifer

Just do it. "I often can't tell what makes me do things. Sometimes I do them just to find out what I feel like doing them. And sometimes I do them because I want to have some exciting things to tell my grandchildren."

-- Lucy Montgomery

This is one of my grandma's favorite jokes. Two nuns were shopping in a supermarket and passed by the beer cooler.

"Wouldn't a nice cool beer or two taste wonderful on a hot summer evening?"

The second nun said, "Indeed it would Sister, but I wouldn't feel comfortable buying beer as I am certain that it would cause a scene at the checkout counter."

"I can handle that without a problem" she replied as she picked up a six-pack and headed for the checkout.

The cashier had a surprised look on his face when the two nuns arrived with a six-pack of beer.

"We use beer for washing our hair," the nun said, "A shampoo, of sorts, if you will."

Without blinking an eye, the cashier reached under the counter, pulled out a package of pretzel sticks, and placed them in the bag with the beer. He then looked the nun straight in the eye, smiled, and said, "The curlers are on the house."

Just like his grandmother. "And I love that even in the toughest moments, when we're all sweating it - when we're worried that the bill won't pass, and it seems like all is lost - Barack never lets himself get distracted by the chatter and the noise. Just like his grandmother, he just keeps getting up and moving forward... with patience and wisdom, and courage and grace."

-- Michelle Obama

Selective memory. "A grandmother remembers all of your accomplishments and forgets all of your mistakes."

-- Barbara Cage

Started with a kiss. At my grandparent's fifty-year golden wedding celebration for just our immediate family, I noticed my grandmother giggling to herself, so I asked her why she was so amused.

Still chuckling she said, "Everyone here because of our reproductive organs!"

Die peacefully. When I die, I want to die like my grandmother peacefully in my sleep and not screaming like all the passengers in her car.

-- Anon.

Single parent grandmother. "My grandmother raised five children during the Depression by herself. At 50, she threw her sewing machine into the back of a pickup truck and drove from North Dakota to California. She was a real survivor, so that's my stock. That's how I want my kids to be too."

-- Michelle Pfeiffer, Actress

Riddle. What is the similarity between a grandmother and a website?

A. Both give you cookies.

Inspirational grandmother. Elizabeth Cady Stanton was a major strategist for Susan B Anthony for the women voting rights movement while she cared for her 7 children. She was also a famous grandmother telling them about her fight for equal voting rights for women. She remained an activist for gender equality, inspiring her grandchildren to take the same route. [13]

When you're right, you're right. My grandmother always told me that regardless of what the world gives you, stay humble. Stay strong in your beliefs and be honest. And when you're wrong, be a man and say you're wrong. And be strong when you're right.

-- Charles Bradley, singer

Grandmothers are gifts

Someone to sigh with

Someone to cry with,

To be through smiles and woes.

Someone to talk with

Someone to walk with

Wherever a path in life goes.

A Grandma is a Treasure,

An all-around pleasure,

To share with, to care with, and love.

Wrapped with affection,

And made to perfection,

A Grandma is a gift from above.

-- Anon.

God's sense of humor. "We grow up opposing our parents only to become like them enough to oppose our children who behave as we once did — a reminder of how dreadful we were toward those now-vindicated grandparents. And you thought God had no sense of humor."

— Richelle E. Goodrich, Author

Need a friend? "Grandmothers are everything in life: If you need a friend, grandma is willing to be your best friend ever."

-- Euginia Herlihy

Granddad plays a practical joke on grandmother. "My good wife started reading "The Exorcist" and got totally upset.

"The next morning, she told me the book was so bad, she took it to the beach and threw it in the water at the end of the pier.

"So, I went and bought a copy of it and ran it under the faucet and put it in her nightstand drawer.

"I know I'm going to hell..."

-- Granddad

Mom's job. Mom said to her young ones, "If you think I'm being mean, it means I am doing my job as your mom. If was nice, you would call me grandma."

-- Anon

Love being a grandmother. "I love being a grandmother. That feeling you have for your own child - you don't ever think it will be replicated, and I did wonder if I would have to 'pretend' with my grandchildren. But my heart was taken on day one."

-- Joanna Lumley, Actress, author, activist, presenter

Pretty on the inside. "Being pretty on the inside means you don't hit your brother and you eat all your peas - that's what my grandma taught me."

-- Lord Chesterfield

"Grandma effect" The unique psychological benefits of having grandparents care for a child when parents can't is referred to as the grandparent effect. Studies have shown this has a major benefit to the child." [14]

Other studies have linked grandparents' care to better grades and fewer behavioral problems.

A study at Johns Hopkins found that children are half as likely to suffer injuries under a grandparent's care. Other studies have linked grandparents' care to better grades and fewer behavioral problems.

"For a long time, there's been a fairly controversial debate going on in child welfare circles about where to place children," according to Dr. David Rubin, a pediatrician at the Children's Hospital of Philadelphia who has studied the child welfare system and, in his opinion, children should be placed with their relatives. [15]

Thinking of leaving some thoughts behind? "I wish my mother had left me something about how she felt growing up. I wish my grandmother had done the same. I wanted my girls to know me."

-- Carol Burnett, Comedian, actress.

Doesn't spare words. "I took my grandmother, who hardly ever says a mean word, to the Princess Diana exhibit in Atlanta. When she saw a picture of Prince Charles, she turned to me and said, "That man fell down the ugly tree and hit every branch on the way down."

Autumn face. "No spring, nor summer hath such grace. As I have seen in one autumnal face."

— John Donne

Late. "My grandmother had a friend who was always late. He was late for everything. When he comes in late, he routinely jokes, "Well as long as I'm not late to my own funeral."

"He passed away and there was a good number of people waiting in the chapel for the funeral to begin. They waited for 45 minutes past the time the funeral was supposed to begin.

"Then the funeral director announced that the hearse was stuck in heavy traffic due to an accident and the hearse had his body in it. So, it turned out he was in fact late to his own funeral."

-- Anon.

Always thinking. "A Grandmother thinks of her grandchildren day and night, even when they are not with her. She will always love them more than anyone would understand."

-- Karen Gibbs, Author

Unconditional love. "I know what it is like to be brought up with unconditional love. In my life that came from my grandmother."

-- Andre Leon Talley, Editor-at-large, Vogue Magazine

Grandma married her fiancé's brother instead. "Grandma Bertha was an attractive blonde Norwegian girl who immigrated to New York in about 1910 because as the oldest daughter of a large family she couldn't stand helping her mom raise all her brothers and sisters anymore.

In New York, she met my grandpa, Walter, also an emigrant but from England, who was totally smitten with her. But grandpa was some years older than her, and as a coarse ex-soldier (Boer War, Royal Horse Artillery), he thought he just wasn't good enough for her.

So, he introduced her to his younger brother, who recently arrived from the UK. The two of them became engaged, and grandpa who set the whole thing up, married someone else.

Grandma and her beau started making wedding plans. Fred moves up to Canada to buy a farm, while she returns to Norway to collect her trousseau.

While Fred is in Canada, the first world war breaks out. As people did at the time, he enlists, but in a Canadian regiment. He unfortunately died in the Somme in 1916, as the story goes, shot through the bundle of letters from grandma which he kept under his shirt.

Grandma kind of went off the deep end after that. The letters, with blood and bullet hole were returned to her, and she wore them on a ribbon around her neck in mourning for quite some time.

Grandpa, still madly in love with her, then decides to divorce his first wife to marry grandma. Such a scandal! I do not know why grandma agreed, but she did. By mom's account, the love in that marriage all seemed to be one-sided. Grandma never wanted to be a mother, and always blamed grandpa for 'getting her drunk that night', resulting in my mom. Grandma was always a bit of an unstable person - there were numerous stories about her - and who can blame her, I guess.

I remember one evening a couple of weeks before grandma's death (at age 93 in 1977), mom returned from a visit to grandma with a very strange look on her face. Mom had to explain about her weird interaction with her mother that evening. It seems grandma beckoned her daughter to come close, then whispered to her daughter 'I love you.' Mom was in shock. It was the first time in her life that her mother said that to her."

-- Anon.

Keeping the love alive. After 65 years of marriage, my grandma still calls grandpa "honey," "sweetie," "baby," and "sugar." I asked her for the secret to keep love alive so long.

She said, "I forgot his name 10 years ago, and I'm afraid to ask."

-- Anon.

Finding justice. "Granny always said finding justice was as tough as putting socks on a rooster."

-- Jessica Maria Tuccelli, Southern novelist

Riddle. Why do grandmas not like stairs?

A. They suspect them as they are always up to something.

Parents view. "Every parent knows that children look at their grandparents as sources of wisdom and security."

-- David Jeremiah, American conservative evangelical Christian author

Grandchild's sixth sense. "Something happened to me at the precise moment that my grandmother died. She was three time zones away, but that didn't matter. I believe that I felt something at that moment she passed... some bit of her mortality slipping away."

-- Zak Bagans, Actor

"Paw Maw" is defined as a woman who proudly proclaims her children's dogs as her granddogs.

-- Unknown

Things to do with grandchildren. Give them a sense of identity and complete a family tree. Tell them stories about the family they will remember all their lives.

Tell them stories and share your adventures when you were a child. Ask them to share their stories.

Show them a family recipe especially for a dessert or a pie.

Share your favorite card games or other games and ask them about their online games.

Show them your garden and how to grow a vegetable garden and create their own food.

Play dress up. This is a lot of fun especially if you've kept old clothes. They will love the new experience. Everything old becomes new again!

Grandkids love to see how people live in the past. Take them to a museum or any old-time attraction and it usually fascinates the young.

(By the way, if you want to learn ways to give kids a more balanced life between physical activities and screen games, TV, etc. check out, "Brilliant Screen-Free Stuff to Do with Kids A Handy Reference for Parents & Grandparents" available on Amazon and in bookstores.) [16]

To the point. Grandmas have been known to go straight to the point without even hesitating despite how harsh what she is about to say – just telling it like it is. Here are a few examples. [17]

- In college, I visited grandma and asked her to teach me how to knit. She did and said, "This will be good for you since it will keep your hands busy, so you won't eat so much."

- Grandson: (in grandma's home) "It's hot in here."

Grandma: "You better start going to church since it's a lot hotter in hell."

- Grandson: (coming out as a gay) "I'm gay."
  Grandma: "Yeah, I always knew girls weren't going to like you."

- Granddaughter painting her nails. Grandma stoops over and looks at them and says, "That's a nice shade of whore red."

Love. "Grand motherhood initiated me into a world of play, where all things became fresh, alive, and honest again through my grandchildren's eyes. Mostly, it retaught me love."

-- Sue Monk Kidd, Writer

A joke. The grandparents were visiting their grandson and before going to bed grandpa found a Viagra packet in the grandson's medicine cabinet. He asked him if he could use one.

"Sorry, grandpa, I don't think that would be a good idea. They are very strong and very expensive."

"How much are they? Grandpa asked.

"Ten dollars a pill."

Grandpa thought about it then said, "That's fine. I'll leave $10 under the pillow before we leave early in the morning."

Later the next morning, the grandson got up and found $110 under the pillow. He called grandpa. "It was only $10? Why did you leave $110?"

"I know. The hundred dollars was from grandma."

Ripping advice. "Make up your mind to this. If you are different, you are isolated, not only from people of your own age but from those of your parents' generation and from your children's generation too. They'll never understand you and they'll be shocked no matter what you do. But only your grandmother would be proud of you and say, 'There's a chip off the old block,' and your grandchildren will sigh enviously and say: 'What an old rip Grandma must have been!' and they'll try to be like you."

— Margaret Mitchell, excerpt from "Gone with the Wind"

Grandma sets an example for her grandchildren. Marie Curie won the 1903 Nobel Prize for Physics and the 1911 Nobel Prize for Chemistry and was known as the "Mother of Modern Physics."

She was a grandmother whose grandchildren and their descendants turned out to be illustrious scientists who continue to contribute in different ways to society. Albert Einstein said she was the only person he knew that could not be corrupted by fame. [18]

Acceptance. "Our grandchildren accept us for ourselves, without rebuke or effort to change us, as no one in our entire lives has ever done, not our parents, siblings, spouses, friends and hardly ever our own grown children."

    -- Ruth Goode

The same person in different roles.

My mom as a mom, "You get what you get. Deal with it."

My mom as a grandmother, "Would you like your grilled cheese cut in hearts or little stars, dear?"

    -- Anon.

Lived with my grandmother. "The very rough story is this: I'm a Melbourne boy, out of both my parents' houses at a young age, so I lived with my very encouraging grandmother and a drama teacher who twisted me into doing this TV thing that I thought my mates were doing, too."

    -- Ben Mendelsohn, Multi-award-winning actor

Grandma and the Bible. Every time a little boy went to a playmate's house, he found the friend's grandmother deeply engrossed in her Bible. Finally, his curiosity got the better of him. "Why does your grandmother read the Bible so much?" he asked.

"I'm not sure," said his friend, "but I think she's cramming for her finals."

-- Anon.

The secret to long life. "Grandma, you are 105 years old, what's the secret for such a long life?" her grandson asked.

"Simple" she replied, "I don't have enough money for burial services."

Florida. "The best babysitters, of course, are the baby's grandparents. You feel completely comfortable entrusting your baby to them for long periods, which is why most grandparents flee to Florida."

-- Dave Barry

A few stories about my grandma. My Grandma was Polish and very aggressive. Once her cousin had a coat that was coming apart. This made her mad and she bullied him into giving it to her to take back to the department store. He told her they probably would not take it back. She marched in and they replaced it with a new coat. He thanked her but said it would have been Ok— the coat had been 20 years old.

My Grandma chased the runaway family dog so it wouldn't get lost and carried George home through the streets of Brooklyn covered in the pile of poop she found him rolling in.

She once chased off a mugger by beating him off with a newspaper.

When my dad had acne and she could not afford to treat it, she sympathetically told him "If they don't like your face, tell them to look at your ass."

Finally, she refused to compliment the ugly baby of a neighbor but congratulated her on her beautiful... baby carriage.

-- Anon.

Great-grandma's recipe. "I have my great grandmother's recipe for black beans, all the way from Cuba, and I know how to make those. I'm actually pretty good at it now. But my first time, the beans actually exploded in the pot, so I had black beans just dripping from the ceiling - which is actually a dream come true for most Cubans. It was a nightmare to clean."

-- Danny Pino, Actor

Creating memories. "Grandmothers are like magicians. They can create wonderful memories for their grandchildren out of thin air."

-- Anon.

Choice of words. Little Johnny and grandpa were in a supermarket when Johnny yelled out, "Grandpa, I need to pee!"

"We are in a public place, don't say you need to pee, say something nice, say you need to sing."

Later, when grandpa was sleeping, Johnny went to grandpa's room and woke him up, "Grandpa, I need to sing!"

Half asleep, grandpa said, "It's midnight, you can't sing now."

"But I need to sing really bad!"

"Well ok then. Sing quietly to grandpa's ear."

Dancing. "I am grateful to those who are keepers of the groove. The babies and the grandmas who hang on to it and help us remember when we forget that any kind of dancing is better than no dancing at all."

-- Lynda Barry, Cartoonist, author, and teacher

Sounds like a what? "My grandmother and I were in Walmart when we were looking at dog toys (she enjoys spoiling my parents' dog). I was kind of meandering when I looked behind me and noticed my grandmother was hunched over with tears falling to the ground.

I immediately ran over because I thought something was wrong, but when I got to her, she was holding this squeaky pig and all she could muster out between breaths was, 'It sounds like a FART!'

So, for the next 10-minutes, my grandmother and I stood in the aisle laughing til we cried because this toy pig sounded like a fart." [19]

Definition of Fun maw. Like a regular grandma only more fun.

    -- Unknown

Fire hydrants. A grandmother was delivering her grandchildren back to their parents one day when a fire truck zoomed past. Sitting in the front seat of the fire truck was a Dalmatian dog.

The children started discussing the dog's duties. "They use him to keep crowds back," said one child.

"No," said another. "He's just for good luck."

A third child brought the argument to a close. "They use the dogs," she said firmly, "to find the fire hydrants."

Cigars. "My grandmother was the only grandmother I ever met who smoked cigars."

-- Roald Dahl, Author

Viewpoint. "If your baby is 'beautiful and perfect, never cries or fusses, sleeps on schedule and burps on demand, an angel all the time,' you're the grandma."

— Teresa Bloomingdale, Author

Top secret. "What happens at Nana's... stays at Nana's."

-- Anon

Another one of my grandma's favorite jokes. A farmer named Clyde had a trailer accident. In court, the trucking company's overly aggressive lawyer was questioning Clyde.

"Didn't you say, at the scene of the accident, 'I'm fine,'?" asked the lawyer.

Clyde responded, "Well, I'll tell you what happened. I had just loaded my favorite cow, Bessie, into the..."

"I didn't ask for any details", the lawyer interrupted. "Just answer the question, ...please. Did you, or did you not say, at the scene of the accident, 'I'm fine!'?"

Clyde said, "Well, I had just got Bessie into the trailer behind the tractor, and I was driving down the road...

The lawyer interrupted again and said, "Your Honor, I am trying to establish the fact that, at the scene of the accident, this man told the Highway Patrolman on the scene that he was just fine. Now several weeks after the accident he is trying to sue my client. I believe he is a fraud. Please tell him to simply answer the question."

By this time, the Judge was fairly interested in Clyde's answer and said to the lawyer, "I'll allow it. I'd like to hear what he has to say about his favorite cow, Bessie."

Clyde thanked the Judge and proceeded. "Well, as I was saying, I had just loaded Bessie, my favorite cow, into the trailer and was driving her down the highway when this huge semi-truck and trailer ran the stop sign and smacked my John Deer Tractor right in the side. I was thrown into one ditch and Bessie was thrown into the other. I was hurting, really bad and didn't want to move. However, I could hear old Bessie moaning and groaning. I knew she was in terrible shape just by her groans."

"Go on," the judge said.

"Then shortly after the accident a Highway Patrolman came on the scene. He could hear Bessie moaning and groaning, so he went over to her. After he looked at her, and saw her fatal condition, he took out his gun and shot her between the eyes. Then the Patrolman came across the road, gun still in hand, looked at me, and said, 'How are you feeling?'"

"Now tell me, what the heck would you say?"

Skip generations. "They say genes skip generations. Maybe that's why grandparents find their grandchildren so likeable."

— Joan McIntosh, Actress

Money's worth. "Grandmas don't just say 'that's nice' — they reel back and roll their eyes and throw up their hands and smile. You get your money's worth out of grandmas."

-- Anon

Grandparents have more financial control than most. You probably already know this. Grandparents control 75% of the wealth in the US. And after working their careers, they have the highest average net worth of any other age group and 55% no longer carry a mortgage. [20]

Heroes. "Grandparents, like heroes, are as necessary to a child's growth as vitamins."

— Joyce Allston, Author

Senior driver. Off on the side of the road, a police officer is checking his radar for speeders and notices a car with 4 senior women traveling very slowly down the highway. He turns on his emergency lights and pulls them over and as he walks up to the driver's window, he can't help but notice the rest of the women in the car are white as a sheet, staring straight ahead with their mouths open.

"What's the problem, officer?" the driver asks.

"Sorry to stop you Ma'am but you were going too slow and going too slow is just as dangerous as speeding too fast."

"But officer, I was going the speed limit. I was driving at exactly 19 mph, she said proudly."

"Ma'am 19 mph isn't the speed limit. That's the sign to tell you are on Highway 19."

Embarrassed, the driver grinned then politely thanked the officer for pointing that out.

"Before I go, Ma'am, I couldn't help but notice the other ladies in the car seem to be in some kind of shock? They haven't said anything at all. Are they, okay?"

"Oh, they'll be alright in just a minute, officer. We just got off Highway 129."

A gift. "Grandmothers are a gift not to be taken lightly. So many lose them, before they are old enough to know their magic. I am glad my bones were born with this knowledge. She taught me how to become a good ancestor. At least this - loving her presence, appreciating her wisdom - is something I know how to do well."

— Nikita Gill, Poet, and writer

Stable. "Young people need something stable to hang on to a culture connection, a sense of their own past, a hope for their own future. Most of all, they need what grandparents can give them."

-- Jay Kesler, Educator, and University Chancellor

Grandma's house rules.

Cookies for breakfast are acceptable

Parents by appointment only

Only believe half of what grandpa says

Bedtime is negotiable

The word "no" is not in our dictionary

Expect to be spoiled.

-- Anon

Grandma's smile. "A grandma is someone who's dear in every way. Her smile is like the sunshine that brightens each new day."

-- Unknown.

Tell me a story. "Grandma, tell me a story and snuggle me with your love. When I'm in your arms, the world seems small, and we're blessed by the heavens above."

— Laura Spiess

Only then. "When the child you love has a child you love with all that is within you. Only then will you know just how grand being a grandparent truly is."

-- Unknown

Visiting grandmother. A grandmother was giving directions to her grown grandson who was coming to visit with his wife. "You come to the front door of the apartment complex. I am in apartment 14T. There is a big panel at the door. With your elbow push button 14T. I will buzz you in. Come inside, the elevator is on the right. Get in, and with your elbow hit 14. When you get out, I am on the left. With your elbow, hit my doorbell."

"Grandma, that sounds easy, but why am I hitting all these buttons with my elbow?" the grandson asked.

"You're coming empty handed???"

"Every house needs a grandmother in it."

-- Louisa May Alcott

Famous people raised by a grandmother. Did you know these people were raised by their grandmothers?

- Maya Angelou

- Carol Burnett

- Eric Clapton

- Bill Clinton

- Bobby Darin

- Willie Nelson

- Jack Nicholson

- Barack Obama

- Oprah Winfrey

It's not too late to start. Great-great-grandmother, Edith Murway-Traina is the oldest woman powerlifter according to the Guinness Book of World Records. She's 100 years old and lives in Tampa. She can lift 140 lbs. She said years ago, she went into a gym and, "I saw all these other ladies lifting weights, and it looked interesting. I picked up a couple of weights and had to prove to myself that I could accomplish this."

A friend of hers said, "You can't drag Edith anywhere. She kept going because she always keeps going. She will not quit, and anything that's hard... that makes her more determined. If it's easy, she might get bored, but if it's hard, she's going to do it. Nobody's going to tell her, 'Oh, that's too hard for me.'" [21]

Dr. Granny. "When Granny was headed for some far-off place, you could only be sure of one thing: that it was a place everyone else was trying to get away from.

"And if anyone asked her why she was doing it, she'd answer, "I'm a doctor, for God's sake, and ever since I became one, I've not allowed myself the luxury of choosing whose life I should be saving."

-- Fredrik Backman, Swedish author, and columnist

Grandma tells it like it is. "Oh, Zoeybird, did I call your mother's husband a damn turd monkey out loud?"

"Yes, Grandma, you did."

She looked at me, her dark eyes sparkling. "Good."

— P.C. Cast, an excerpt from "Chosen"

Seriously, "Grandparents should play the same role in the family as an elder statesman can in the government of a country. They have the experience and knowledge that comes from surviving a great many years of life's battles and the wisdom, hopefully, to recognize how their grandchildren can benefit from this."

— Geoff Dench, Professor, and social scientist

Treasure. "Grandparents are a family's greatest treasure, the founders of a loving legacy, The greatest storytellers, the keepers of traditions that linger on in cherished memory. Grandparents are the family's strong foundation. Their very special love sets them apart. Through happiness and sorrow, through their special love and caring, grandparents keep a family close at heart."

-- Anon.

My eyes! "Unfortunately, my grandparent's house burned in a house fire one night. It was horrible, and most of my family turned out the next day to help them. My 90-something grandmother was standing in the front yard telling my cousin and me the story of what had happened the night before.

"Then your grandaddy ran out in nothing but his thongs!"

(She was referring to his shoes, but the visual was still more than I was ready for.)

-- Anon.

Grandmother . . .

Has ears that truly listen

Arms that always hold

Love that's never-ending

And a heart that's made of gold

-- Unknown

Popular grandmas.

- Asks rather than answers

- Gets silly

- Avoids grandparent rivalry

- Is totally mellow over messes

- Does things – instead of just giving things

- Is not a burden

- Avoids playing favorites

- Takes the lead

- Is always a grandchild's confidante

- Stores and shares family memories

Indian chief. "My grandmother was in the hospital after having a colonoscopy and resting and flatulated loudly. A nurse came in right then and my grandmother apologized.

'It's alright. No worries. It actually means I'm doing my job properly. It's a feather in my cap,' the nurse said.

We all chuckled as my grandmother replied to the nurse, 'Thank you, and if you work a long shift, I might make you an Indian chief.'"

    -- Anon.

Magician. "Your grandma is a magician. Remember that time when you fell off your bicycle and she lifted you up onto the kitchen counter? She cleaned your bloody knees, washed the tears and snot off your face, told you funny stories, and tickled your stomach until you giggled so hard it made you hiccup. The tears, the blood, the pain, your mum's closed bedroom door—all vanished as if your grandma had waved a wand—sim sala bim!

"Hard to keep your smile off your face now, no? She did such things. Still does. A trickster, she is. Always full of pranks and laughter...

Like now ... Bet she opens her eyes any moment now with that mischievous grin of hers, pleased she fooled you. You'll both double over in laughing fits."

-- Margrét Helgadóttir, excerpt from "Grandma's Tricks"

A hug. "Some moments can only be cured with a big squishy grandma hug."

— Dan Pearce, Single Dad Laughing

My grandmother is 95, and very religious. My 6-year-old son was simply curious about her age, and this was their conversation. By the way, my son doesn't know the Hansel and Gretel fairy tale.

Grandson: Grandma you are 95! That is a lot!

Grandma: Yes, it is!

Grandson: Most people die before they are so old, Grandma.

Grandma: Well, most people don't cook small children in the oven and eat them. It's the secret to long life.

Grandson: MOM! GRANDMA EATS SMALL CHILDREN! THATS WHY SHE'S SO OLD! Don't eat me, Grandma!

Grandma: Only kidding, dear.

We hope you enjoyed our book!

If you liked our book, we would sincerely appreciate your taking a few moments to leave a brief review.

All the best to you and all your family!

TeamGolfwell and Bruce Miller

About the authors

Bruce Miller. Lawyer, a businessman, world traveler, golf enthusiast, and Golf Rules Official, actor, shrewd gambler, whiskey connoisseur, and author of over 40 books, a few being Amazon bestsellers, spends his days writing, studying, and constantly learning of the astounding, unexpected, and amazing events happening in the world today while exploring the brighter side of life. He is a member of Team Golfwell, Authors, and Publishers.

TeamGolfwell are bestselling authors and founders of the very popular 200,000+ member Facebook Group "Golf Jokes and Stories." Their books have sold thousands of copies including several #1 bestsellers in Golf Coaching, Sports humor, and other categories.

Index to paragraphs

We Want to Hear from You!

"There usually is a way to do things better and there is opportunity when you find it."
- Thomas Edison

We love to hear your thoughts and suggestions on anything and please feel free to contact us at Bruce@TeamGolfwell.com

Other Books by Team Golfwell and Bruce Miller

For the Golfer Who Has Everything: A Funny Golf Book

For the Mother Who Has Everything: A Funny Book for Mother

For the Father Who Has Everything: A Funny Book for Father

Dragonflies: A Novel Based on What Men Think of Women

Beware the Ides of March: A Novel Based on Psychic Readings

The Funniest Quotations to Brighten Every Day: Brilliant, Inspiring, and Hilarious Thoughts from Great Minds

Jokes for Very Funny Kids (Big & Little): A Treasury of Funny Jokes and Riddles Ages 9 - 12 and Up

Brilliant Screen-Free Stuff to Do with Kids: A Handy Reference for Parents & Grandparents!

Jokes for Very Funny Kids (Ages 3 to 7): Funny Jokes, Riddles and More

And many more here

[1] Science Daily, https://www.sciencedaily.com/releases/2021/11/211116201530.htm

[2] Ibid.

[3] Pew Research, https://www.considerable.com/life/family/surprising-facts-about-grandparents/

[4] Alegrecare, https://www.alegrecare.com/single-post/2018/05/07/The-Importance-of-Honoring-Your-Grandmother-on-Mothers-Day

[5] Vanessa LoBue, Ph.D., Psychology Today, https://www.psychologytoday.com/us/blog/the-baby-scientist/201811/the-grandness-grandparents

[6] Ibid.

[7] Ibid.

[8] Guinness World Records, https://www.guinnessworldrecords.com/world-records/oldest-first-time-grandmother

[9] Unijokes, https://unijokes.com/joke-1003/

[10] Wikipedia, https://en.wikipedia.org/wiki/Mary_Shelley

[11] Guinness World Records, https://www.guinnessworldrecords.com/world-records/most-living-generations-(ever)/

[12] Caraday Health, https://caradayhealth.com/fun-facts-about-grandparents/

[13] Wikipedia, https://en.wikipedia.org/wiki/Elizabeth_Cady_Stanton

[14] Grandparent effect, ABC News, https://abcnews.go.com/Health/story?id=6199776&page=1

[15] John Hopkins study, ABC News, https://abcnews.go.com/Health/Healthday/story?id=6171563&page=1

[16] Brilliant Screen-Free Stuff to Do With Kids: A Handy Reference for Parents & Grandparents! > https://www.amazon.com/Brilliant-Screen-Free-Stuff-Kids-Grandparents/dp/B0863TW78X

[17] Brutally honest grandmothers, https://www.boredpanda.com/unfiltered-grandmas-stuff-grandmothers-

---

say/?utm_source=google&utm_medium=organic&utm_campaign=organic

[18] Wikipedia, Curie Family,
https://en.wikipedia.org/wiki/Curie_family

[19] Supra. Reddit.

[20] Supra. Pew research.

[21] Guinness World Records,
https://www.guinnessworldrecords.com/news/2021/8/99-year-old-competitive-athlete-become-the-worlds-oldest-powerlifter-670268